Basford
- village to
suburb.

by
Alfred S. Bowley

ISBN 1 874754 24 1

1998

The Nottinghamshire Heritage Series

Happy Walking International Ltd.,
Unit 1, Molyneux Business Park,
Whitworth Road,
Darley Dale, Matlock,
Derbyshire.
DE4 2HJ

Happy Walking International Ltd.,
Unit 1,
Molyneux Business Park,
Whitworth Road,
Darley Dale,
Matlock,
Derbyshire
DE4 2HJ
Tel/Fax 01629 - 735911
E-Mail - john.merrill@virgin.net

Printed, bound, marketed and distributed by Happy Walking International Ltd.

© Text - A. S. Bowley 1998.

First Published - February 1998.

ISBN 1 874754 24 1

British Library Cataloguing-in-Publication Data. A catalogue record of this book is available from the British Library.

Typset in Times - bold, italic, and plain 11pt, 14pt and 18pt.

Cover design © Happy Walking Ltd. 1998.

ACKNOWLEDGEMENTS

Having come into local history late, very late, I have to acknowledge my appreciation of the help I have received from the County Local Studies Library, the University of Nottingham Local History Department and the County Records Office. Arthur Oscroft, formerly Director of Housing for Nottingham also made available his personal and departmental records.

From the Basford Local History Society I have received encouragement and permission to use some of their photographs. Permission to use other photographs and maps has been given by the Nottinghamshire County Council, Leisure Services Department. Other people whose names are mentioned have also kindly provided photographs.

Finally, Terry Fry reviewed my work with a stern and professional eye, but I nevertheless accept responsibility for the final result.
A.S.Bowley.

Any profits from this publication to the Basford and District Local History Society.

CONTENTS

PREFACE

The aim of this book is to present an outline of the history of Basford from the earliest times to 1997. Into this framework may be fitted detailed studies of the areas I have only touched upon, such as buildings, businesses, people, their work, customs and leisure.

Some aspects are already covered in detail: Keith Train on the parish church; Terry Fry's book on Sherwood, and Basford Rural District Council by Geoffrey Oldfield, Maurice Caplan's studies of the Poor Law in Nottinghamshire bring in Basford workhouse. George Murfet has researched hosiery finishing whilst the growth of the lace trade described by David Lowe and Jack Richards provides a background to Basford's industrialisation.

Robert Mellors' *"Old and New Basford. Then and Now"* together with Thomas Bailey's *"Annals of Nottinghamshire"* were useful sources. *'Byestander'*, the magazine of Basford Local History Society has been invaluable as have numerous publications ranging from parish magazines to Professor Beckett's Centenary History of Nottingham.Inevitably the history of Nottingham has to be mentioned Basford being one of its largest satellites. As the parish has been developed and redeveloped it has been necessary to identify earlier sites with present-day locations.

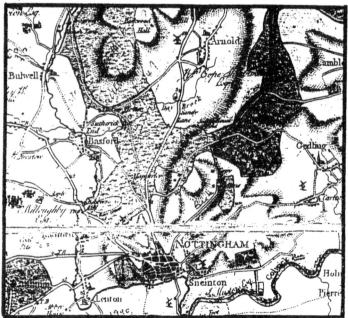

Basford, Near Nottingham - Chapman's Map of Nottinghamshire, 1774.

Chapter One
Origins of the Settlement

The Romans, crossing the great flood plain of the Trent at Barton-in-Fabis on their way west to Derby, also branched north along the high ground parallel with the swampy Leen valley and built a fort near an Iron Age settlement at Broxtowe. Across the valley, on the Mapperley hills near Dorket Head, other Roman traces have been found and it is tempting to believe these invaders made their way between the two sites along the line of the present roads. An obvious route would lead down from Broxtowe to the Leen ford, now bridged at Southwark Street, and thence along Arnold Road and Oxclose Lane. Only in recent years have our rivers been confined to regular channels and, near the Leen valley especially, people would have to live and travel on the higher ground.

Coming from the north-east, after the Romans had departed in the 5th century, the Saxons did not find either the Leen or Trent a barrier. They settled on the present Lace Market hill in Nottingham and placed a branch of their local government - The Hundred - again at Broxtowe. Later still, in AD 868, the Danes used the Trent as their highway and occupied the Saxon site in Nottingham. Also at Broxtowe, the Danes collected their taxes from the people living to the north of their town and in the Leen valley

The Hundred they renamed the Wapentake, but the original name was later revived and remained in use until 1894.

Although Broxtowe was so important in Roman, Saxon and Danish times, and the place where the men of Basford would swear allegiance and pay their taxes, the only traces of earlier habitation there are those of the Iron Age village and the Roman camp. These were discovered in 1937 when the ground was being cleared for the building of the present Broxtowe Estate. Broxtowe Hall itself was demolished about the same time and only a piece of its wall with a gateway, near the Bells Lane traffic island remains

On the other hand, Basford was a substantial settlement in Saxon times and has continued to be so. Its existence is due to its position on the route from Nottingham to Mansfield in the north and Derby to the west. Until the coming of the Normans in 1066, Nottingham was settled on the present Lace Market hill with Stoney Street its main road through the town. Travellers heading from this early borough for the north or west could avoid the very steep hill from Chapel Bar to Canning Circus by using tracks along the line of North Sherwood Street or Mansfield Road. The height of the cliff faces left of Derby Road and right of Wollaton Street show how much has been now cut away to reduce the gradients. From the present Gregory Boulevard junction the road north lay up Sherwood

Rise and down Nottingham Road, known as Sandy Lane until a century ago. At the bottom of the hill it met the barrier of the Leen and Day Brook which joined close by the present railway footbridge near Nottingham Road. This low-lying area from Bacon's Field to Vernon Park was known as Myrey Close or Muddy Field in present day terms. As late as the 19th century nearby plots were shown on leases and deeds as Boggy Close, Bottom Close and Gravel Close and this junction of the two rivers was still subject to flooding until the 1960s.

To avoid this marsh the road forded the Leen and headed for the higher ground beyond. It continued along the line of the present Lincoln Street and went on up David Lane heading eventually for Ilkeston and Derby, or Alfreton.

A branch of the track at David Lane forded the Leen again and headed for Arnold, Bestwood and Bulwell. In bad weather when Lincoln Street and the Basford end of Nottingham Road were flooded a third ford over the Leen was needed. This was at the present Church Street and led to Alpine Street (formerly called Backside) and Percy Street high above the flooding.

On the hillside between Lincoln Street and Percy Street grew up the settlement, later to be known as Basford Town and by the last-mentioned ford, in the 12th century the parish church was built, probably on the site of an earlier chapel where travellers from Nottingham emerging from the forest could find shelter and food.

The name Basford, spelt in several ways from early times, could mean the lower ford although Keith Train, the prominent local historian, also suggests it could have been derived from Basa's ford, named after some Saxon landowner. Percy Street recalls the family name of the Dukes of Northumberland while Lincoln Street, formerly known as Town Street, is named after Lord Lincoln, the title of the eldest son of the Duke of Newcastle, one time Lord of the Manor.

The Leen fords at Lenton, Radford, Bobbers Mill and Mill-in-the Hole were probably less important in early times than those at Basford, again because of the the steep Derby Road and, being lower down the river were probably more subject to flooding.

Cattle from Derbyshire to Nottingham were certainly driven through Basford, taking a break on the journey beside the stream at Stockhill. Their destination was the Nottingham cattle market then at Burton Lees, where the Guildhall stands on Burton Street.

Stone from Basford Quarry, off Tilbury Rise, was much used in Nottingham and would most likely have been taken over the same route. For example, the Broxtowe Hundred was responsible for maintaining three of the Leen Bridge arches on the London Road and in 1368 stone from the quarry was used in a new tower at Nottingham Castle.

Because the Basford area has been developed and redeveloped intensively over the centuries any archaeological evidence of its history has been lost, although, of course there may have been none in the first place. Roman coins have been found at two places in New Basford, but these are not really significant.

Little recorded evidence is available about the parish during the turbulent Saxon and Danish times. Nevertheless, as the Domesday Book lists no less than five mills on the Leen in Basford only twenty years after the Normans arrived it seems likely they served a substantial farming community.

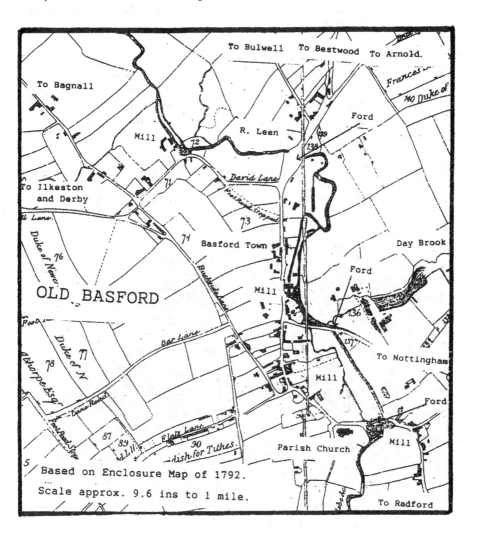

Based on Enclosure Map of 1792.
Scale approx. 9.6 ins to 1 mile.

An idea of the people of Basford at the time of the Norman invasion in 1066 can be gained from the Domesday Survey of 1086. Having taken control of England and decreed that its wealth belonged to the Crown, William the Conqueror sent commissioners to list his spoils. He gave Basford to his son, William Peveril, whose mother was the wife of one Ranulph Peveril another member of the Norman invasion. William Peveril must have served the Conqueror well as the parish was only one of fifty-five he received together with a number of houses and other property mainly in Nottinghamshire and Derbyshire. He built no residence in Basford, but controlled his estates from his castles in Nottingham and at Castleton in Derbyshire.

He established a court, The Honour of Peveril, at Nottingham Castle to administer these holdings. Much later this Court was to be based at Basford and have responsibility for a very wide area but the lack of a resident Lord of the Manor meant no powerful figure was watching the parish interests. The Domesday Book lists six manors or farms in the parish, probably on the high ground of Whitemoor and Stockhill.

The land east of the Leen was more of a sandy nature. There, bounded by that river, the Bestwood hills, and the Mapperley Plains lay the Basford part of the famous Sherwood Forest which stretched from Nottingham to Worksop.

Mill Street Mill, damaged by fire 1938.

10

The Domesday Book also mentions five mills at Basford. There are still traces of four undershoot water mills where the Leen formerly flowed. The first is now a ruin on Mill Street. It worked until 1938 when it was seriously damaged by fire. At that time it used a turbine, a horizontal water- wheel well remembered by local people because of the noise it made. The second mill was on Lincoln Street opposite the bottom of Cowley Street and a third was down a cul-de-sac beside the Fox and Crown public house on Church Street. A fourth mill was Mill-in-the- Hole at the southern extremity of the parish. 'The church mill' probably disappeared when the railway line was laid. Five mills for grinding grain indicates a substantial farming community in 1086 but the parish did not grow larger for seven hundred years.

Basford Parish Church

The Parish Church of St Leodegarius.

The Domesday Book mentions the presence of a priest on the land of Saxfrid, one of William's followers.Although Basford's first parish church was built on the present site by Saxfrid's son Robert in 1126 it is likely that this priest's chapel was established there much earlier. The church is dedicated to St Leodegarius, a martyred bishop from central France probably chosen to recall Robert's family connections with that country.

Keith Train's book on the history of the church gives a detailed description of it as it was up to 1969. Although the church no longer marks an exit from Sherwood

Forest, its elegant tower still stands at an important centre of communications. The river, railway and the road from Nottingham to Bulwell run side-by-side past the church whilst thousands of motor vehicles stream past day and night on the city's ring road level with the roof of the nave.

Some of the points Keith Train makes in his book bring out matters best seen in the context of their times. Although Henry V111 proclaimed himself Head of the Church of England and broke the tie with the Pope in 1534 in all other respects he accepted the doctrines of the Roman faith. He died in 1547 and during the short reign of his son, Edward V1, church buildings and rituals were drastically altered.

For example, traditionally, only the clergy and the more important people took Holy Communion in parish churches throughout the year and then it was taken out of sight behind the rood screen separating the nave from the chancel. The rest of the congregation were informed that communion was being taken by the ringing of a bell. A 'Pax' was then passed round for them to kiss. Usually the 'Pax' was an icon in wood, silver or ceramics. In Basford it was different. Pope Innocent 1V (1243 to 1254) blessed a square tablet of porphyry, a volcanic rock, and this was Basford's 'Pax'. When, under Edward V1, the whole congregation was allowed to take communion the rood screen and the 'Pax' were abolished.

High above the chancel arch, remain the stone brackets on which the rood screen had rested four centuries ago. During building work on the church in 1858 plaster was removed from the eastern jamb of the south door and the Basford 'Pax' was revealed set in the stone work. Whilst most other 'Pax' have been lost, it seems this had been hidden there. Its position suggests that those in the congregation who wished to continue kissing the icon could do so on entering the church as is still a common practice in some Greek Orthodox churches.

When Henry V111 came to the throne in 1509 Basford church had in its square, squat tower a bell bearing the mark of Richard Mellors who had died two years earlier. His foundry was on Long Row in Nottingham. The bell bears the inscription 'Sancta Maria' and has survived all the changes of the Tudor years and the centuries since.

In that time it has served the community by calling the faithful to prayer, giving warnings of emergencies and celebrating national events.

By 1552 the church had three bells, two of which were replaced in the early 17th century. These two were melted down to become part of a new peal of eight bells cast in 1921 as a memorial to the 210 young Basford men killed in the Great War. The Mellors bell now rests in the nave of the church.

One has to sympathise with the parishioners of those Tudor years when dramatic changes took place under Protestant Edward followed by his staunch Roman Catholic sister, Mary. Churchgoers must have wondered what new would be facing them, especially as the penalties for failing to conform were so severe.

And what of the clergy? Service rituals changed, buildings were altered, one day priests could marry, the next it was forbidden! Whatever their problems, a story must lie behind the brief ministries of Robert Moore (1550 - 1551); Richard Hill (1551 - 1552) and Christian Tynmore (1552 - 1563).

Justices and Churchwardens

From Norman times day-to-day administration of country parishes was in the hands of the church if there was no resident lord of the manor. The priest with his churchwardens were responsible for the church buildings, highways, the poor, and the Peace. Some parishes still have Churchwardens' Accounts giving a good insight into parish life. Unfortunately those for Basford are not to hand. They may have been destroyed or perhaps they rest among the private papers of one of the great landowners who bought and sold plots in the parish. Records of Basford baptisms, marriages and burials survive from 1561 though, and, coupled with Archdeaconry Records hold information about the church and parishioners.

The churchwardens would bring minor offenders before the justices who usually heard cases at their homes or in a local public house. They were not required to keep records. The Basford lock-up and stocks were at the junction of Alpine street and Church Street, conveniently opposite the White Swan public house. In 1842 the stocks were last used for a drunken man who had caused a disturbance in the church. He was only kept there for two hours. The more serious cases were tried at Quarter Sessions or the Assizes. The County Archives Office holds these records.

Sherwood Forest at Basford

In 1154 Sherwood Forest was designated a royal reserve and made subject to the Forestry Laws which made taking game or timber without authority punishable with death. According to the Thoroton Society's recently published "*Sherwood Forest in 1609*" it seems it was never densely wooded. From the earliest times the Basford section now known as Sherwood, Mapperley Park, Carrington and New Basford was a sandy waste of ling and gorse. No doubt any trees there may have been were taken as fuel or for timber-framing the mud-and-wattle houses of the town. On 8 January, 1795, John Aspinall, an American travelling from Nottingham to Mansfield complained 'This is the first Forrest I ever saw without trees. I believe we rode six or seven miles without seeing a single tree which I thought an odd thing in a Forrest'

Some farming was allowed on parts of the forest. One manor house was that of Algarthorpe on the east bank of the Leen where Egypt Road now meets Radford Road. In 1330, this house was owned by William Eland then deputy to Richard de Grey of Codnor, the Governor of Nottingham Castle. Richard de Grey was at that time fighting in France and Eland held the castle keys. The King, Edward 111, had only recently reached the age of eighteen and his mother, the widowed Queen Isabella with her lover, Roger Mortimer, Earl of March, was ruling the country from Nottingham Castle. They were popular in Nottingham having gained a Charter for the townspeople, but their arrogance led to opposition from other nobility. The king decided it was time to assume his authority and sent a messenger to Eland demanding access to Nottingham Castle. Without doubt, Queen Isabella had agents among the king's followers because she sent for Eland's keys. It is said, she slept with them under her pillow thereafter. Nevertheless, Eland assured the messenger he knew of a secret way into the castle.

On 18 October, 1330, the king and his party arrived at Basford and joined Eland. Soon after midnight that night they set off. Their route is not known, of course, but to avoid the town it seems likely that they followed the course of the Leen down Plantation Side, through Radford and Lenton to the foot of the castle near Brewhouse Yard. There Eland opened a door to a storehouse in the base of the castle rock and from the back of this cave they climbed a passage up to the inner bailey high above. As the party emerged through a door there they were challenged by two sentries who were immediately slain. The guard turned out, but when the young king made himself known they accepted his authority. Despite his mother's protests, the king ordered Mortimer to be arrested, and taken to London. There, he was tortured, briefly tried and taken to Tyburn to be hanged, drawn and quartered. The king sent his mother to be detained at Castle Rising, near King's Lynn where she stayed until her death at the age of 65 years. It is said he visited her there from time to time.

Because of the risks he had taken, Eland was rewarded with a knighthood and a seat in Parliament. He was also granted the Honour of Peveril which he removed from Nottingham's Shire Hall to Basford where it eventually became responsible for 127 parishes in Nottinghamshire and 120 in Derbyshire, Leicestershire and south Yorkshire, including Rotherham and Sheffield.

Part of its civil court work was the recovery of small debts and the maintenance of debtors' gaols. The long-established Fox and Crown public house on Church Street, formerly known as The Bowling Green, was one of Peveril's prisons and remained so until 1790 when the White Hart at Lenton became the debtors' prison. Apart from a brief spell in a house on St Peter's Street, Radford, (opposite Skill's garage) the prison remained at Lenton until the Honour of Peveril was abolished on 31 December 1849.

The Fox and Crown, Church Street, formerly 'The Bowling Green'

Eland received the Honour of Peveril in 1336 and it is not known where was his first prison, but it was in the cellars of the Bowling Green inn for many of the following 500 years that the Court existed. Eland Street marks this phase in Basford's history.

Cloud on the Horizon?
Queen Elizabeth (1558 - 1603) brought a measure of religious stability to the country during her long reign. No doubt some of the parishioners at Basford had been disturbed by the conflicting doctrines filtering down from far-off London. Others had simply conformed to the changes in order to survive. Now, six miles away at Calverton, the rector, William Lee was experimenting with a machine which would change the whole appearance of the parish and influence the lives of all who would later live in it.

Chapter Two
The Arrival of Industry

For centuries weaving and handknitting had been the means of producing material from wool, flax, silk and cotton thread. In colder climes both sexes and all social classes wore thigh- length hose hand-knitted by countless numbers of men and women. William Lee's machine was aimed to carry out this task. He took his model to London where, it is said, Queen Elizabeth refused to approve it on the grounds that it would cause widespread unemployment - a factor still important today - so Lee went to Calais where it had a limited success.

Lee's brother later brought an improved version of the invention back to this country and by the turn of the 18th century the knitting industry was established in London. Trading problems there, however, caused it to move back to the East Midlands, where it had all begun. Leicester concentrated upon woollen hose, Derby on the silk trade and Nottingham on cotton.

Nottingham was particularly fortunate in that, in the middle of the 18th century, James Hargeaves and Richard Arkwright, both inventors of spinning machines set up businesses in the town. The combination of the knitting frame and mechanised cotton spinning brought work and prosperity for some. Such was the influx of workers from the farms and villages surrounding Nottingham hoping to benefit from this prosperity that the need for building land became critical.

Until 1700 when Nottingham's population was 5950 the town had been seen as a 'garden city' with mansions for the gentry and an important social life based on the ducal palace which had replaced Nottingham Castle. It was all to change and with it life in Basford.

By 1750 Nottingham's population had nearly doubled to 10,910 and by 1790 it had increased again to 24,400. But the living and working space for all these extra people remained the same. Inevitably many of the gentry moved from the town to the country. Their houses were pulled down or sold to become warehouses. Workshops and back-to-back houses filled their former gardens and all other available land. Soon parts of pleasant Nottingham were reduced to slums where poverty, sickness and discontent made it a national disgrace.

In 1740 Thomas Langford, Mayor of Nottingham,a former goldsmith, made Basford House his country home, possibly tempted to move there by the news that one Henry Ward of the Tinker's House on Arnold Road had only recently died having lived in Basford to the age of 109 years.

There was room for development within the town boundary. Three large open spaces of common land could have been made available for the much-needed housing and factories. This land was, however, controlled by the town's burgesses who had grazing and other rights there. These rights they obstinately refused to give up.

This affected Nottingham's neighbouring parishes. Lenton, Radford and Sneinton, the nearest, were soon being industrialised. A Scot named Robertson, later calling himself Robinson, built mills beside the Leen at Bulwell and at Papplewick, whilst Basford, much of it nominally royal forest, began to feel the impact.

Early Hosiery Finishing at Basford.

It was the practice, called crofting, to lay fabrics out in the sun for bleaching, a lengthy process for which there was no space in Nottingham. Basford had this space. More important the waters of the Leen, the Day Brook and in the sandstone beneath were ideal for washing and dyeing the finished product. As early as 1609, Richard Bankes' map shows some development along the Day Brook and either side the road to Radford. By 1790 the Day Brook was dammed in three places. One was near its junction with the Leen and traces of it can still be seen behind the present Vernon Road Bleaching Company. This reservoir served a bleach yard in Myrey Close owned by Robert Hall (senior), his son, also Robert Hall, John White, and John Lever.

Nottingham Journal report on 13 February, 1790: *"Whereas the bleaching grounds of Hall and White of Basford near Nottingham were robbed last night of a quantity of ribbed and plain cotton hose, nearly white: This is to give notice that any person who can give such information (shall receive a) reward of ten guineas and a pardon for King's Evidence."*

The same newspaper reported the death of a well-known local bleacher, Andrew Pearson, In 1810, Robert Hall, (senior) and John Lever having died, Hall, (junior), sold his share to John White. Streets nearby are named after White and his manager, Amos Fox.

There was a second dam upstream on the Day Brook near the present junction of Valley Road and Barlock Road and a third belonged to Jonathan Farrand whose bleach yard is now the site of Petworth Drive playing field. This factory was demolished in the 1930s to make way for the Heathfield Estate.

By the 1790s the numbers of houses in the High Street (Basford Road) area; near the ford to Bulwell, then known as Sutherick End; and along Lincoln Street had increased to accommodate more workers. Apart from a few scattered farm buildings mainly in the Bagnall Road area, Basford was still sparsely populated. On the eastern border of the parish though, along the Mapperley Hills Road, (now Woodborough Road) Thomas Oakland had built a brick kiln in 1761 and great clay-pits were being dug to provide bricks for the new buildings in Nottingham.

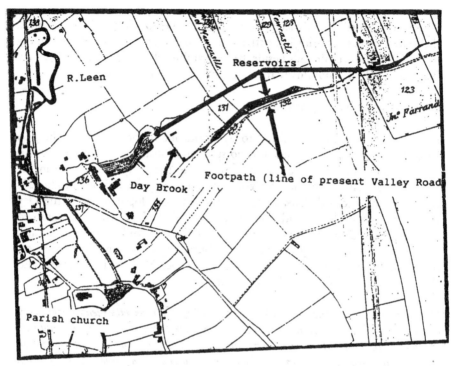

Bleach yard reservoirs on the Day Brook c1792.

Mapperley Park

The hillside in the south-east of Basford parish, adjoining the Nottingham boundary, was known as Corner Wong when it was bought in 1396 by a wealthy wool merchant from Mapperley near Ilkeston. Over the centuries it changed hands many times but by 1792 it was owned by Ichabod Wright, a banker of Nottingham. In 1792 a start was made on building his mansion, Mapperley Hall and the parkland around it took on the name. There is a stained glass window to his memory in the parish church. His bank, now part of Lloyds, is on Carlton Street in Nottingham.

The Hall family

Having sold his interest in the bleachyard at Myrey Close, Robert Hall, junior, bought land called Raw Wong in 1810 from the Duke of Newcastle. It lay at Town End, now the junction of Bagnall and Cinderhill Roads and there was a brickworks on the site. There he built Basford Hall. He and his family made important contributions to industry during the century. In addition to his bleachyard he was engaged in cotton-spinning and was one of the first to use chloride of lime for bleaching as a substitute for 'crofting'. He died in 1827 at the age of 71.

His son, Samuel experimented at his works at Two Mile Houses, Nuthall Road, introducing the 'gassing' of yarn - passing the thread through a flame to remove loose fibres. This was important when the lace trade built more intricate machines producing finer work. He also developed a starch which his brother Lawrence marketed at home and abroad.

Another son of Robert Hall was Marshall who became a prominent physician noted for his opposition to 'bleeding' as a treatment. He was a physician at the General Hospital in 1825 and when he died in 1857 at the age of 67 he was interred at the General Cemetery.

Turnpike Roads

Throughout the 18th century industry was demanding improved communications. Privately funded toll-roads, turnpikes, received Parliamentary approval to solve this problem. Country lanes and tracks linking towns and villages were improved and new highways were cut to make more direct routes just as motorways were to do some two hundred years later.

Some turnpikes had a direct impact upon Basford. The Nottingham to Newhaven turnpike (1758) now Nuthall Road replaced Whitemoor Road from Bobbers Mill through Basford to Nuthall. The gradient of Derby Road from Chapel Bar to Canning Circus was greatly reduced at the expense of Lord Middleton to facilitate the turnpiking of the roads to Trowell (1763) and to Derby (1780). These were needed to bring coal from the developing mines of the Erewash valley and lead from south Derbyshire. Some of this heavier traffic had been taking the longer route through Basford.

Finally, the Nottingham to Mansfield turnpike, passing between Bestwood Park and Arnold was started in 1787 and with the reducing of the climb at Red Hill provided a shorter route than the traditional one following the valley of the Leen.

At that time Basford had no coal mines and so was not linked to the growing network of canals in the area. The nearest canal was cut from Cossall to the Trent picking up coal from Wollaton Pit. The Leen itself, of course, was not navigable in the parish area.

Chapter Three

Basford Enclosure of 1792

If Basford was no longer an important staging post to the north and west of Nottingham it still had considerable natural resources ripe for exploitation beside its open lands and fine water supplies. The forest had long since given up its timbers and for centuries its massive quarry at Cinderhill had supplied building stone for the area. This was now giving way, however, to brick, with the raw material coming from the clay pits of Mapperley.

The western boundary of Nottingham covered the edges of the Derbyshire coalfield. Although these resources were tapped at Wollaton and Strelley, no pit was to be sunk in Basford for many years to come.

On the 7 and 14 January, 1792 the Nottingham Journal carried a brief announcement on its page 4 from John Renshaw, a solicitor, of Owthorpe. Anyone interested in the enclosure of the open lands of Basford was to meet at the Blackamore's Head inn, Pelham Street, Nottingham on 17 January.

Further meetings were held and on 25 August following Mr Renshaw published a notice on behalf of the Enclosure Comissioners that a final chance to submit a claim would be held at the White Lion inn, Long Row on 25 September.

Throughout the nine months of meetings there was no public protest at or welcome for the enclosure, no demonstrations, nor comment in the press. Yet a centuries- old way of life was to change. Further the Basford section of Sherwood Forest was to be enclosed. England was moving from an agricultural-based economy to one based on industry and the new towns. Probably even the poorer people of Basford thought they might benefit.

The Nottingham Common Council expressed no opinion but instructed its clerk and a small committee to make sure that the boundary between Basford and the town was properly drawn. It seems the council was not interested in absorbing this wide area and taking on its potential adminstrative problems

By the end of the year, 1792, the Enclosure Act was passed to be followed by a map showing the names of those who had secured plots.

As Lord of the Manor, the Duke of Newcastle was well- represented having chosen sites his successors would know as the Aspley, Whitemoor, Heathfield, and Stockhill council estates. He also received part of Sherwood and a triangular piece of land, bounded by Hucknall Road and Sherwood Rise close to the boundary with Nottingham. Within a few years Nottingham businessmen and managers were to live on this south- facing slope.

Robert Smith, a banker, was allocated plots at Carrington, a name he adopted when he was enobled. Henry Cavendish received lands further north along the Mansfield turnpike soon to become a suburb of Nottingham in its own right. White's Directory of 1848 declared Carrington to be an area 'for good class residents', and Sherwood 'the most elegant suburb in the Nottingham area.'

The Sherbrooke family were allocated the site of the future Sherwood estate and other plots were taken up by the Earl of Chesterfield, Lord Middleton and Jonathan Sherwin. Members of prominent Basford families, Jeffrey Brock and Jonathan Farrand were allocated plots as were others some of whom are recalled in street names. Rawson, Athorpe, Pearson, Huthwaite, Beardsley, Sanders, all appear on the map as does Anna Gawthern, whose name lives on, mispelt, in Gawthorne Street.

The vicar of Basford was awarded a substantial field on the hillside rising from the Day Brook to Bestwood Park and now covered by the City Hospital. This was for his tithes.

Commissioners also laid down the routes of the most important roads in the parish. They are Arnold Road, Park Lane leading to Bestwood, Broxtowe Lane, Bells Lane, Sandy Lane (now Nottingham Road), Hall Lane (now Radford Road), Hucknall Road, and Red Lane (now Redcliffe Rd). This last-named formed the parish boundary with Nottingham. It was the main road from Nottingham to Lambley until the lower part of Woodborough Road was built in 1848.

The Nottingham to Mansfield turnpike was already approved and the various widths, forty or fifty feet were specified.

Although the enclosure meant that much of the land at Basford had been allocated and could be used no immediate development took place.

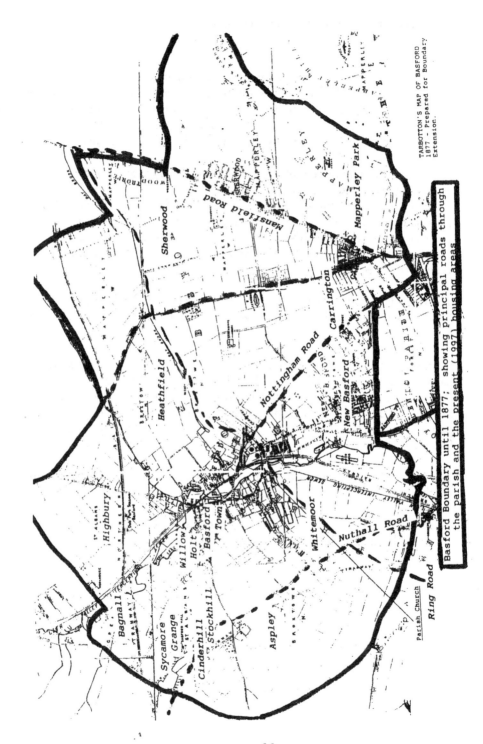

TARBOTTON'S MAP OF BASFORD 1877 - Prepared for Boundary Extension.

Basford Boundary until 1877; showing principal roads through the parish and the present (1997) housing areas

22

As they went into the 1800s the 2000 people then living in Basford must have noticed little had changed after the enclosure. However, much was happening elsewhere, which would transform their way of life.

In Belper, the Strutt family had brought workers from their scattered workshop-cottages to spin cotton and silk in a 'manufactury' where machines were powered by water from the Derwent. This factory idea was taken up in Nottingham, but with men and horses providing the power. The steam engine was still being developed.

Workers in Nottingham were living in tenements, usually built in squares with some twenty families sharing one tub lavatory and water was sold at a farthing a bucket. Thus sickness through malnutrition, overcrowding and unhealthy living conditions meant that few survived beyond their twenties. Conditions in the town were a scandal, Because the council would not release land for building more and more workers moved out to the nearby parishes.

At Basford, houses were specially built to take the knitting frames and some still survive to be identified by the wide top-floor windows giving the maximum daylight. The knitter usually rented his frame and his wife worked beside him to mend, shape and sew the garments he produced. Their children, from the earliest age, were kept close by to fetch and carry. These long hours of hard physical labour were needed to provide a bare living wage. Many must have wondered whether their move from farm-work had been worth while.

Among those moving into the towns were former blacksmiths and wheelwrights. These were to become the mechanics, the backbone of the new industries. When trade was slack they adapted and modified their frames to improve the product. John Heathcoat, in 1809, adapted a frame to make twist lace. A little later, John Levers developed a net machine. With others, their inventions laid the foundation of a new industry for Nottingham, machine-made lace.

The Luddites

The hosiery trade had always been volatile. When trade was slack, fierce competition arose between the self-employed worker with his rented frame and the master-hosiers with their 'manufacturies'. When there was no work, the latter would pay off their workers with garments from stock instead of wages. This was known as 'truck', and many years later was made illegal. Another cause for unrest was manufacturers who turned to making 'cut-ups'. As the name implies, inferior hosiery products were cut, shaped and sewn from plain material, a cheaper method of production against which the individual worker could not compete. Many were brought to the point of starvation.

As a result knitters banded themselves together, using the collective name of 'Luddites'. During 1811 and 1812 they systematically damaged the frames of those they considered to be the worst employers. Basford was quickly drawn into this conflict where a leader was James Towle living at New Basford, then a small group of houses on the Radford Road. Press reports of the day, describe the rioting and framebreaking at this time.

During the summer of 1811 frames were broken at Arnold, Kimberley and Bulwell forcing the hosiers to take their machines to safer places in Nottingham. On a Tuesday in November a cart carrying eight or nine frames was being driven through Basford when masked men attacked the load, breaking the machines with heavy hammers. Again, on 23 November, 1811 workshops were attacked in Basford, some thirty frames were broken and the pieces scattered about the streets.

Parliament was so concerned that about 800 cavalry, including The Royal Horse Guards and a detachment of Dragoons with a thousand infantry were stationed at the barracks on Derby Road and in billets round about. Inevitably by the time the troops arrived on the scene the rioters had usually dispersed. Rewards up to £500 were offered for information leading to the arrest of those responsible but without success. Two detectives from the London Bow Street Runners were sent to help trace the ring-leaders but again the identity of the offenders could not be discovered.

On 17 March 1812, at the Nottingham County Assizes two young Basford men, William Carnel and Joseph Maples were convicted of breaking seven frames on the premises of John Braithwaite at Basford and each was sentenced to fourteen years transportation to Australia.

On 27th April following 'two very small men' attacked a Mr Trentham, a wealthy frame-owner, in Kayes Walk near St Mary's Church in Nottingham. One of the men shot him in the chest with a large horse-pistol. A reward of £600 was offered but, again, despite this large sum no information was forthcoming. No doubt many suspected the offenders were two Basford men, one of them, James Towle.

The usual sentence for framebreaking was transportation to the colonies, but the increasing use of firearms by the Luddites caused the Lord Lieutenant, the Duke of Newcastle, to call for the death penalty. This was introduced in 1814.

On 12 January 1812, frames were broken at Radford and Clifton. Thomas Bailey reports. *"The same evening two soldiers were stationed in the house of a person named Barnes, at Basford, to assist him in the protection of his machinery; but while they were sitting by the fire , with their arms resting near them, seven men rushed in and seized them."*

WHEREAS,

Several EVIL-MINDED PERSONS have assembled together in a riotous Manner, and DESTROYED a NUMBER of

FRAMES,

In different Parts of the Country:

THIS IS

TO GIVE NOTICE,

That any Person who will give Information of any Person or Persons thus wickedly

BREAKING THE FRAMES,

Shall, upon CONVICTION, receive

50 GUINEAS

REWARD.

And any Person who was actively engaged in RIOTING, who will impeach his Accomplices, shall, upon CONVICTION, receive the same Reward, and every Effort made to procure his Pardon.

☞ Information to be given to Messrs. COLDHAM and ENFIELD.

Nottingham, March 26, 1311.

G. Stretton, Printer, Nottingham.

25

These Luddites, broke three frames and then made off with the soldiers' muskets.

One of the most violent Luddite incidents occurred in October, 1814, again at New Basford. Following an attack on a house when several frames were broken, the occupier, a man named Garton gave information that James Towle was one of those responsible. Towle was committed for trial and on 14 October Garton heard that his own life was in danger. He took refuge in Nottingham and his wife went to stay next door with a Mr William Kilby. After dark, several armed policemen hid in Garton's house and about half-past nine three men entered followed by several others. They heard a noise from the officers' hiding place and fired two or three shots towards them, but without causing injury. The police responded by firing a blunderbuss, killing the leading intruder. The rest fired again but then ran from the house. Mr Kilby, in the next house, hearing the noise opened his door to be confronted by one of the Luddites who pushed a pistol in his face and shot him dead.

Next morning, the body of the Luddite killed in Garton's house proved to be Samuel Bamford, a boyhood friend of Towle. Both he and Towle were very small men. Although a large reward again was offered for information connected with the murder of Mr Kilby, nothing came to light. Towle was acquitted of the charge for which he had been arrested. There can be no doubt that, whether through fear or loyalty, no-one was prepared to give evidence. Witnesses and juries were probably intimidated but such were the terrible working and living conditions at the time that much public sympathy lay with the Luddites.

One young man, William Felkin, later to be an important figure in Nottingham, was employed to ride round the workshops of certain employers to offer better conditions to the knitters there when it was learned that attacks on their machines were likely.

Towle eventually suffered for his crimes. At midnight on Friday 28 June, 1816 some men attacked the lace factory of Heathcoat and Boden at Loughborough. Three guards there were attacked, a blunderbuss was fired at one of them named Asher wounding him seriously in the head. The Luddites then went up to the first floor where they overpowered four men working. They damaged twenty-five machines on that floor and thirty more on the floor above. Five workers there were threatened with death The Luddites then made off, after telling the wounded Asher that they hoped he would soon get better.

On this occasion Towle had been careless. He had allowed a silk handkerchief across his face to slip during the attack and Asher was able to identify him. Further, on the way back home to New Basford Towle met the Basford Constable, Benjamin Barnes, riding through Beeston on his way to intercept the offenders. Towle's shoes were wet, so it was assumed he had crossed the Trent by the ford, and he was detained.

At the Assizes on the 10 August Towle was convicted of aiding and abetting the firing of a pistol at Asher and was sentenced to death. He was hanged at Leicester County Gaol. It was reported he conducted himself with dignity to the end.

Master-Hosiers, Bleachers and the 'Better-off'

If the Basford workers found the new century hard, there was another way of life in the parish. Ichabod Wright's mansion was completed in his parkland at Mapperley. Robert Hall, junior was at Basford Hall, Thomas Bailey, owner of the Nottingham Mercury newspaper was compiling his Annals of Nottinghamshire soon to be published from his home at Basford House. Algarthorpe Hall had long been replaced by Bagthorpe House, situated at the top of the present Quorn Road. It was owned by the Duke of Newcastle, was the centre of a large farm, and in 1844 was rented by Lieutenant John White, adjutant of the Nottinghamshire Yeomanry and four years later by Mr G.A.Morrison. Well-known bleachers such as Pearson, Cox, Bexon, Fox, Farrand, and others were well-established and living near their businesses. They were soon to be joined by Henry Ashwell and the new lace-makers. Nottingham factory owners and their managers were building homes on the slopes of Sherwood Rise and at Sherwood itself.

Coach parties regularly drove out from Nottingham to the Bowling Green. The debtor/prisoners formerly in the cells at this public house were no longer there to serve their ale having moved to Lenton, but the players could still enjoy their game in the fresh air and pastoral scenery beside the Leen at Church Street. The parties at the Bowling Green, by now called the Fox and Crown, were not always so pleasant, though. Thomas Bailey reports an incident in his 'Annals'.On 1 January, 1806, a number of young army officers on recruiting duty in Nottingham gathered at the inn. One of them, a member of the Hall family, fostered a quarrel between two of his companions, a Lieutenant Browne and an Ensign Butler. They sent for pistols, retired to a secluded part of the grounds with their seconds, and Browne was killed. He was carried to the parish church and later buried in St Mary's churchyard in Nottingham. The inquest returned a verdict of murder. Butler and the seconds were never traced. Hall returned years later but was never prosecuted.

New Basford

On 5 May, 1815 Mrs Abigail Anna Gawthern sold one of her plots of land, that at the junction of Town Street (Lincoln Street) and Nottingham Road to a Mr John Sanders, but most of the land- selling was five years later between North Gate and Beech Avenue.

Heathcoat's patent for lace making expired in 1820 resulting in a trade boom. Over the next two years terraced houses for some 2000 people were built in this area to a standard high for the time. Some are still providing acceptable accommodation today.   In among the houses were built a wide range of workshops, factories and warehouses, mainly off-shoots of Nottingham businesses. New Basford had now become a feature on the map in its own right.

Richard Birkin

Among the local framework-knitters at this time was Richard Birkin. In his teens he had left his home in Belper for Nottingham. He was to become a leading industrialist, found a dynasty and become Mayor of Nottingham. In 1825, his talent for hard work brought him a partnership with a Nottingham alderman named Biddle They built a factory on Mount Street, New Basford. It was 1841 and Birkin was still only twenty years old. Taking every advantage of new developments, they introduced twelve machines driven by steam, the first in the area. They still had, however, twenty hand-knitting frames which were to remain in production for some years to come.

Maud Street, New Basford

Basford Workhouse

In 1814 the Basford Poor Law Incorporation was formed comprising forty parishes in the Broxtowe Hundred and in Derbyshire. The next year, the Basford Workhouse was built on the boundary adjoining Bulwell, the site of the present Highbury Hospital. It was to be one of the biggest institutions for the relief of the poor in the area.

Thousands of workers with their families but with little or no capital were still leaving the land looking for work in Nottingham and the surrounding industrialised villages. They brought with them a heavy burden of sickness and destitution which the parishes had to deal with. In 1834 the Basford Union was formed and by 1842 the workhouse had been enlarged to hold 370 people from a population of 51,794 in its forty-three sponsoring parishes. The government did its utmost to reduce the numbers eligible for parish help by restricting admissions to the workhouse to the 'able-bodied destitute'. The incoming population, deprived of family support of their home villages, had to turn to the parish when they were in distress. Between 1846 and 1870 93% of the workhouse inmates were children, the aged, or the sick.

Such were the harsh conditions imposed by the commissioners from central government that chairmen of the management committee sometimes felt impelled to resign rather than agree to their policies. On the other hand, when a hospital for the mentally ill was opened at Nottingham, the Basford Union did not transfer those who were eligible because they themselves could keep these patients more cheaply. The Basford Union grew sufficient vegetables on land at the workhouse to feed its inmates with a surplus for sale. This idea was copied at other workhouses.

Credit was due to Basford employers in one respect. They did not employ London orphans in their factories and work them to death as was the case elsewhere in the County.

Education

Education did not become compulsory until 1870, but the churches had been arranging classes for many years although parents had to pay a few pence. There were also a number of dame and small private schools. One of these was established in 1832 in Mill Street by a Mr T. Troughton whose advertisement in Lascelle and Hagar's Directory of 1848 read *"The pupils of this school are carefully instructed in a liberal education to commercial and professional pursuits, also civil engineering."* His terms were : Board and education 18 to 26 guineas per annum; Day pupils 15 shillings to two guineas per quarter; Boarders were limited to ten. Academy Place on Mill Street was a reminder of this school until Basford Town was demolished.

The 4th Duke of Newcastle succeeded to the title and Lordship of the Manor in 1831. In 1843, at the request of the vicar, Rev. Robert Simpson he gave about one and a half acres of land on Church Street for a new cemetery as the churchyard was full. He also gave a plot opposite the White Swan, for a National (church-sponsored) school with places for 450 boys and girls whose parents paid a small fee. The parish lock-up and stocks had been removed from the site only two years earlier. This school was used for youth groups and Sunday Schools until it was demolished about 1960.

Nearby, at the post office on Church Street, Mr Twells the postmaster kept a lending library of 300 books.

Basford Workhouse - Original Block.

Chapter Four

Parliamentary Reform

The Reform Bill of 1831, aimed at giving more property-owners the vote, failed to pass through Parliament. The Duke of Newcastle had opposed the Bill and when riots followed in Nottingham, his mansion, the Castle, was set on fire and looted. Basford men were said to have been involved. When the courts ordered compensation to be paid for the damage, Nottingham Town Council declared the building to be outside its jurisdiction. The costs therefore fell upon the Broxtowe Hundred of which Basford was a part.

A new Reform Bill in 1832 was passed and gave a few property owners in Nottingham a vote as did a further Act in 1835, but no immediate change came to the general situation, particularly in the parishes. The Nottingham burgesses who had had control of the town for generations continued to use their influence. Despite further government reforming legislation and more centralised control including ordering enclosures which released more common land for building, progress was very slow. Public disorder, cholera, and trade fluctuations were major problems in Nottingham during those middle years of the 19th century. The town now had a population of about 50,000, and Basford more than 6,000. Many of the newcomers came from outside.

Thomas North

In 1842, Thomas North, a mine-owner with a pit at Babbington, near Kimberley, opened up a new colliery at Cinderhill across the road from Basford Hall where he later took up residence. The colliery was a model of its time with many advanced ideas. Basford had missed the boom in canal building, so North constructed a mineral line to move his coal, first by horse-drawn wagons later using steam engines. His line ran parallel with Nuthall Road, turning to follow the route of the present ring road to Wollaton. There, close by the Crown traffic island, a wharf was built on the Cromford canal. The line also served the Newcastle pit when it was opened soon afterwards opposite the bottom of High Street (now Basford Road). North named his Cinderhill pit, 'Babbington Colliery'.

He also built terraces of houses for his workers, one at Cinderhill itself, Holden Square, and another, Napoleon Square near Broxtowe Lane. This last square was cut in two to allow his mineral line to pass through. North also developed much of Cinderhill in those years and was elected Mayor of Nottingham in 1844 celebrating his appointment with a grand ball in the town. He also made substantial contributions to Christchurch at Cinderhill. He was highly regarded at the time and when he died in 1868 at the age of 57 an obelisk to his memory was placed over his grave at the Church Street cemetery. Unfortunately, he had

31

business problems and by his death he was bankrupt bringing difficulties to fellow investors.

The Railways

If the coming of industry had brought change to the parish in the 1820s, the 1840s were equally important. Coal was in demand for the growing use of steam power and domestic heating throughout the country. The turnpikes and canals could no longer cope. To protect their interests, the canal owners managed to keep the main railway line to the north out of Nottingham, so the lines went through Derby and the engineering works were also built there. In 1839, however, a branch line was accepted from Derby through the Meadows to a station in Carrington Street. From it, in 1848, a branch to Mansfield was opened along the Leen valley. Its effect on Basford was dramatic.

This line was laid within a hundred yards of the parish church bringing a level crossing beside the stone Leen bridge, only built in 1832. A small station and goods yard with their noise and smoke were established beside the garden of Basford House. The Nottingham Road entrance to Basford Town and the northern exit at David Lane now had level crossings to contend with as well as fords.

Babbington pit was soon linked to this line.

William Scaling

A trade booming in Basford at this time was wickerwork. The main producer was William Scaling who planted extensive groves of willows beside the Leen at Mill Street. His works and 'manor house' were on Bagnall Lane. He introduced a wide range of basket-work which was displayed at the Great Exhibition in 1851 and was honoured with the Royal Warrant. Wickerwork was later produced on a wider scale at factories such as that of Morris Wilkinson on Radford Road near Isandula Road and by individuals working in small workshops. Basford became a major producer for this trade. In the 1920s the trade lost its popularity when the fashion for short skirts meant that wickerwork shopping baskets and furniture laddered women's stockings.

The Police

For more than a century people had moved from their villages and continued to do so in increasing numbers. A result was that they no longer had the personal support and constraints they had formerly experienced. Poverty and crime prevailed to an extent the country had not seen before. Central government responded by replacing the old parish constables with local police forces. The Nottingham force was formed in 1835 and that in the County in 1839. The County Police replaced the Broxtowe Hundred Rural Police in 1845 and built stations for its constable on Radford Road and an inspector on Woodborough Road.

The Churches

A positive response in support of the new unstable population came from the churches. Many non-conformist chapels were built in the industrial parishes such as the first Methodist church built on Stockhill Lane in 1797 and Old Basford Baptist chapel established in 1801. These buildings were often similar in appearance to the factories of many of their sponsors whose names were duly carved on foundation stones.

The parish church of St Leodegarius already had chapels serving in its growing hamlets. A daughter church, St John's was consecrated at Carrington in 1843; Christchurch at Cinderhill in 1856; and St Augustine's, New Basford in 1862.

On 16 September, 1858, the Rev. Henry Pitman called a meeting of 'gentlemen interested in the restoration of the church'. A committee was formed, refurbishing and enlarging commenced. Unfortunately, this effort was hampered when, on Sunday morning, 3 April 1859 the tower fell down narrowly missing the parish clerk. More fund- raising was required but the work was completed by 22 December 1859 when the opening service was to take place. For some reason it was delayed.

As part of the refurbishment a solid fuel boiler was installed in a cellar close by the south porch. This cellar remained dry and in use until the late 1980s when it began to flood. It is significant that Bailey's 'Annals' mentions a holy well in the church yard in 1409. By 1859 industry was taking great volumes of water from beneath the parish and there was no trace of the holy well. The new cellar was dry. By the late 1980s with the departure of most industries the water table had risen and was flooding the cellar which had to be abandoned.

Rev. Thomas Ambler Bolton

This curate at the mother church was clearly a wealthy man. In 1855 he bought Stockhill House on Stockhill Lane together with much of the surrounding farm land. He greatly enlarged and handsomely decorated the house. When New Basford became a separate parish Thomas Bolton was its first priest. He also gave or raised much of the cost of the church building and an adjoining schoolroom, the land being given by the Gawthern family.

At his death in 1868 his wife renamed their home 'Bolton Hall'. Later occupants gave it the name 'Rock House'.

Henry Ashwell

By 1851 the population of Basford exceeded 10,000. There were coal mines at Cinderhill and on Nuthall Road; brickworks also at Cinderhill and at Mapperley enjoyed the housing boom in Nottingham's St Anns and Meadows. The stocking frame, developed to produce a huge range of products, including lace, remained the main industry in the parish, however. It had brought with it machine building, printing, soap making, chemicals, packaging but, above all, dyeing, bleaching and finishing.

A prominent figure in hosiery finishing was Henry Ashwell, born in 1828, son of a Nottingham iron-founder, a leading figure in the town. Ashwell built a bleachyard on Radford Road in 1855. Business success enabled him to build Woodthorpe Grange as a residence in 1870. He was a member of the Basford Local Board and was busy in several other committees which may have led to a decline in his business. It was no longer profitable in 1909 and thereafter changed hands many times until it was finally closed in the 1960s. The building of the suburban railway which passed through the grounds of Woodthorpe Grange caused Ashwell to sell the house and move to Nottingham where he died in 1909. He is buried in the Nottingham Road cemetery.

Shipstone's Brewery

Born in 1822, James Shipstone established his brewery on Radford Road in 1852. He was a strong supporter of the New Basford Wesleyan church.

Shipstone's Brewery, Radford Road.

34

His son, also James, joined the company in 1880 and took over when his father died in 1897. Business was so successful that at one time 185 horses were kept for deliveries. James (junior) died in 1922 and his successor Thomas - later Sir Thomas - managed the firm until his death in 1940. The company was purchased by Greenall Whitney in 1978. The brewery was closed in 1990 and demolition of its extensive site commenced in 1997. The land-mark tower and buildings fronting onto Radford Road remain for the moment.

Basford Gasworks

Coal gas for street lighting had been provided on a limited scale in Nottingham by the Gas-light and Coke Company from the Eastcroft as early as 1819. By the 1850s demand was so great that additional gasworks were built in Radford and Basford. Soon the company was among the largest in the country aiming to supply a wide area outside Nottingham, even as far as Eastwood.

Basford gasworks on Radford Road beside the Leen and the railway line became the main producer. It was also a few hundred yards from the parish church whose stonework and stained glass windows were to suffer from the fumes for the next hundred years. Great clouds of grit would also descend upon nearby housing whenever the management decided under the cover of darkness, to 'clear the retorts'. Typically, in March, 1873 the council received a complaint that the Basford gas-holders 'were becoming rather leaky'. Despite this, local legend was that those living nearby enjoyed good health. They were also able to buy coke for fuel and creosote for their fences at very low rates.

If the people had to endure pollution, the long-serving Rev. Henry Pitman suffered even more in the 1880s. His vicarage stood on the other side of the ford from the church where there is now an ornamental garden. This house was taken into the new gas works for use as an office. The vicar moved across the road, but soon he had to move again as the space was needed for two huge gas-holders. He moved briefly to Springfield House, a mansion on Radford Road close by the present gasworks entrance. This, too was taken over and finally, he moved to a purpose-built vicarage a mile away, on a peaceful site behind the new cemetery on Nottingham Road.

When Nottingham Corporation bought the gas company in 1874 Basford was producing almost as much gas as the Eastcroft and Radford works together. To attract workers for the plant, the Corporation planned a block of flats, called the Albert Buildings, modelled on the Victoria flats in Bath Street, Nottingham. The Basford Local Board at first refused permission for the project but in 1877 gave way, probably because of the impending boundary extension. The site chosen was on Nottingham Road opposite the junction with Scotland Road. People living at the time thought them a joke, lettings were few and the block was demolished. By 1901 all that remained was its front wall and fence. The low brick wall in front of Mann Egerton's car show-room, successor to Flewitt's woodyard, is a reminder of this building. The gasworks themselves, though, were to dominate the heart of the parish until the 1960s when the site became simply a distribution centre for North Sea gas.

In May, 1939 the Germans prepared a war map covering Nottingham and pin-pointing Basford gas-works but it was never attacked.

Water Supplies

Traditionally, Nottingham had relied upon the Trent, the Leen and wells for domestic water supplies. As there were no public sewers in the early 19th century the contents of tub- lavatories were used to manure the fields between the Leen and the Trent. Inevitably the rivers become highly polluted. Industrial development made the situation worse. Two private water companies amalgamated and their engineer, Thomas Hawksley did much to improve supplies. In 1827 three springs on the Scotholme nursery, beside the Leen north of the present Wilkinson Street bridge, were directed into a covered reservoir and piped for the town. Again, in 1857 beam engines were installed on Haydn Road to pump water from the sandstone beneath Bagthorpe Farm. They were housed in a handsome building fronting onto an ornamental lake.

Haydn Rd Water Pumping Station

The Corporation bought the water company in 1879 and retained it until the reforms of the late 1940s. The buildings have gone, the lake is replaced by a car park, and one of the engines now stands in Wollaton Park Industrial museum.

Despite Hawksley's efforts and the Leen Valley Sewerage Act of 1872, the villages upstream of Nottingham, Lenton, Radford, Basford, Bulwell, Papplewick and Linby continued to use the river for their effluent. The problem was solved by the construction of a brick-built intercepting sewer which ran parallel with the west bank of the river, passing close by the parish church tower. By 1880, Basford had a direct link to Stoke Bardolph Sewage Works. Nevertheless, it was time for Nottingham to take over most of the surrounding parishes.

Chapter Five

Nottingham Borough Extension Act, 1877

Many of Basford's industrialists also had interests in Nottingham where some were members of the council. The town also had three dynamic chief officers in addition to Hawksley who worked part-time. Samuel George Johnson was Town Clerk, Marriott Ogle Tarbotton was Borough Surveyor and the Medical Officer of Health was Dr Edward Seaton. The time had come to extend the town boundaries. The Town Council eventually supported a bill to bring into the town Sneinton, Lenton, Basford and Bulwell, Basford covering the largest area. Small areas from other parishes, such as Clifton and Carlton were also included but major land-owners, the Musters, Edges, and Cliftons stopped them going further.

At a final meeting to approve the bill in January, 1877, there was still opposition. Alderman Thackeray who was also Chairman of the Radford Local Board claimed that there had been no demand from the parishes for change, and if the town was made larger it would have to employ higher-paid officials to manage it. In time these would become master of the elected members. He lost on a vote of twenty-six to three but was right in saying that the parish local boards had not sought the move. Indeed there was widespread belief, reported in the *Nottingham Journal*, that Nottingham only wanted the parishes for their income to pay for its new civic buildings.

Nevertheless the bill went through and on 1 November, 1877 and most of Basford's Local Board functions passed to the Guildhall. Its redundant offices on Nottingham Road became reading rooms. Next they were used as a school for children with learning difficulties and in 1958, when the Westbury School was opened, the Haven public house was built on the site.

Basford Rural District Council

When Basford's public services were transferred to Nottingham, the Basford Union was excluded. In 1894 the contributing parishes were taken over by the newly-formed Basford Rural District Council. In 1899 Poor Law in Basford was moved to the borough. The Basford Union and RDC both kept the name 'Basford' in their titles although Basford was no longer part of either. The RDC offices were at Rock House on Stockhill Lane until 1974 when local government was re-organised.

Geoffrey Oldfield's history of the RDC mentions its crest, a shield with three dancing bears. It can be seen on the gable of the Nottingham Road cemetery lodge. Mr Oldfield points out that there is no ancient justification for this crest which was that of a Staffordshire family named Beresford. It is likely Basford never had a coat of arms, the various Lords of the Manor using their own family insignia.

The Close of the 19th Century

There was change in Basford following its loss of independence. Slowly the fields at Sherwood and Carrington were filling with houses. Some, for workers, followed the traditional terrace style of 'two-up-and-two down'. They had a scullery with its own cold water tap, a kitchen, sometimes a 'front room', and a coal cellar. Sewers now allowed for a lavatory in the common yard behind. Similar houses were added at the centre of the parish, mainly in the Southwark Street area, towards the bottom end of Nottingham road and in Vernon Avenue.

New Basford from Fairfax Street (the present Valley Road) to North Gate was completed to the same standard, with some larger houses either side of Nottingham Road. Street names reflected the overseas Empire. Zulu, Suez, Isandula, Rosetta and Chelmsford - a General- commemorated African campaigns.

Parts of Mapperley Park were being developed in the 1880s and road names such as Magdala reflected the Abyssinian campaign of 1860, Cyprus was annexed in 1878 and Lucknow Drive recalled the Indian Mutiny of 1858. Queen Alexandra was remembered by a road in Carrington and Lily Langtry in a Grove at a respectful distance over the hill in New Basford.

Public Transport

Some people still worked close to their homes but others were commuting to Nottingham itself. For some years there had been horse buses from the town to Carrington and in 1874 permission was given for horse-drawn trams to cover the route. In 1876 the Tramways Company was permitted to lay its track from Long Row to Wood Street - later Fairfax Street, now Valley Road. Strange to say, the license allowed them to carry animals, coal and goods not exceeding eight tons. It seems this service, with cock-horses to help climb Derby Road from the town did not operate until 1881.

At Church Street, Basford a substantial bridge was built across the railway and Leen in 1875 but the tram lines went no further than the Shoulder of Mutton public house, now the site of MacDonald's restaurant. Tram sheds were built on Pearson Street and there was grazing for the horses on a field behind on Isandula Road, In 1882 the Corporation experimented with a tram drawn by a steam engine, but it was not approved.

Bulwell needed public transport but the trams could hardly be directed through the narrow Lincoln Street and Bulwell Lane. The railway company agreed to build a road beside their line from Church Street to Southwark Street. The junction they provided was not acceptable and now leads to a car-dismantling yard. Instead Radford Road at the gasworks was realigned and in 1882 the new Vernon Road was driven between the gasholders which had displaced the temporary vicarage. This Basford Town by-pass ran parallel with the railway as far as Southwark Street. There it swung away to join Bulwell Lane at Catchem's Corner. A high stone wall separated the railway and Vernon Road to prevent the trains frightening horses, the main road transport.

At this time most roads in the parish were paved with granite sets, sealed with tar. Where pavements and terrace yards were paved at all, blue tiles with a diamond pattern were mostly used.

In 1899, Nottingham, now a City, having bought the tramways, sent its Engineer to the United States to study their electric trams. By 1901 these were on the routes to Bulwell, Carrington and Sherwood. In 1902 a new route from Queen Street to Nottingham Road was introduced with its terminus at Vernon Road. No public transport was available along Nuthall Road until 1913, Cinderhill people having to walk to Vernon Road.

When the Ripley tram service was introduced it left Nottingham Road onto Church Street bridge, followed Percy Street, Stockhill Lane and crossed the park at Dark Lane to join the Nuthall Road. The trams were open-topped and a dangerous feature on this route was a low railway bridge at Kimberley where the conductor had to warn passengers to lower their heads. The wires and trolley pole dipped close alongside them. The commuting public were also served by the Suburban Railway Line from 1889. This passed along the Great Northern track from a station originally called Dob Park on the embankment at Northern Bridge on Vernon Road. It circled the city through Daybrook and Sherwood to Thorneywood thence to the Low Level Station on London Road. Although it was popular with young people and football supporters, it could not compete with the trams and was finally discontinued in the early 1930s.

The year 1896 found space needed in Nottingham for the Great Central railway line. A large slum area, presently occupied by the Victoria Centre, was cleared and a gigantic hole, some fifty feet deep, was dug to make room for a station with twelve platforms. An hotel and clock tower were built on Milton Street above.

With the 20th Century this new railway arrived in the parish. It entered a tunnel at Carrington where there was a small station, passed under Sherwood Rise to New Basford Station and a goods yard on Haydn Road. It crossed on an embankment to a deep cutting at Perry Road. Thence over the Day Brook valley to the high ground en route for Bulwell and the north. The Day Brook was culverted through the embankment at Farrand's Dam. A footpath beside the Brook also passed through the embankment in a narrow tunnel. Local people used this tunnel to shelter during the Zeppelin raids of the Great War. Few thought that one day it would make way for the four-lane Valley Road.

Widening Valley Road bridge, 1930.

Bagthorpe and the Glebe Lands

In 1889 the vicar of Basford sold his Glebe Lands beside the Day Brook for £27,937 to the Corporation who built an isolation hospital there in 1891. Nearby on Hucknall Road a workhouse was built and opened in 1903 to replace the one formerly at York Street. The whole site is now the City Hospital. Nearer the city, also on Hucknall Road, fields of Bagthorpe Farm were taken to build a prison replacing the old House of Correction. It was opened in 1891.

Bagthorpe Workhouse and Hospital c 1901
(Hedge in foreground follows line of Day Brook)

Fire at St Leodegarius, 1900

The long-suffering Henry Pitman, parish priest, found the new century opening with a disastrous fire in his church. The building was undergoing extensive repairs with Hopewell and Sons as contractors. Early one morning a train driver on the railway nearby called Sgt Harwood from Radford Road Police Station. The City fire brigade under Superintendent Robinson turned out but much of the roof and interior furnishings were lost in the blaze. Most of the cost of restoration was covered by the Lord of the Manor, the Duke of Newcastle. The Rev. Pitman died the following year.

A fourth daughter church was built on Southwark Street in 1910 dedicated to St Aidan. In 1877, the Wright Estate had given a plot of land on Woodborough Road for St Jude's church. Although this was within the ancient Basford parish boundary, it was, in fact, a daughter church of St Anns.

Vernon Park

Vernon House on Vernon Road was the home of Charles Cox, director of Cox and Widdowson whose bleach yard adjoined his extensive grounds. In 1901 he sold this residence with its parkland to the Corporation and moved into Rock House. His former home became a pavilion for a bowling green and the whole estate was opened up as a public recreation ground.

Council Housing(1)

The Corporation introduced a Housing Department in 1910. For the first time the council was planning to house people other than its employees, but the outbreak of war stopped any progress in this direction.

Chapter Six

The Great War - 1914 to 1918 and afterwards

Although Basford suffered no war damage during the Great War, the general public endured considerable hardship from shortages and the absence of their young men in the forces. Of these, 210 were killed in action. Their memorial column stands unnoticed at the top of Nottingham Road cemetery but a book in the nave of the parish church records their names. The Mellors bell and a new peal of eight bells were dedicated in 1922 to their memory. Many of those who did survive were disabled by their wounds or were racked with coughing from the affects of poison gas. The next twenty years were to be marked by a bitter pacifism, unemployment, and disturbing news from abroad.

Yet it seemed a kinder society, family support supplemented by voluntary work was evident. Cricket and football teams played on Vernon Park and on the Mill Street ground. Long columns of cyclists snaked out into the countryside and groups of hikers caught the trains to Edale and other parts of Derbyshire. Children's games cost nothing but effort, and their pocket-money was often based upon the horse-manure they collected from the roads and sold to gardeners. Schools, chapels and churches provided many with holidays through Scouts, Guides, Boys' Brigade, and other groups

Men were still the main support of their families, women being dismissed from employment by the public services and some others on marriage. Absence from work, whether through sickness or bank holiday almost always meant no pay. The Old Age Pension was insufficient to live on and meant that few could ever fully retire.

Light engineering and hosiery still provided much employment although the lace trade continued to decline. Council and work in the public services, the railway, and those with Players and Boots were in enviable occupations. Ex-servicemen had priority for work in the Post Office and the coal-fired boiler-houses of factories and public buildings were usually manned by former stokers of the war-time battleships. Doctors, the clergy and teachers were the most accessible members of 'The Establishment'.

Day-trips to the East Coast by train were a special treat. Whole trainloads of children and helpers went off from Vernon Road station on Sunday School Outings to exotic places such as Codnor Park and Edwinstowe. Near at home, the Bowling Green public house no longer attracted day-trippers, Basford families would take the tram to Wilford, cross the half-penny-bridge and picnic in Clifton Grove or beside the Fairham Brook.

Basford Wakes was held on waste-land between Fairfax Street and Reigate Road where a Harby Street had been demolished. Celebrating the festival of St Leodegarius, the fair should have been held on 2 October, the date of his martyrdom, but it has been moved to the Sunday following the 11 October, no doubt in deference to Nottingham's Goose Fair.

A new Labour Exchange was built on the wakes site in the early 1930s and each Thursday Fairfax Street would be crowded with men 'signing on' for the dole. Those even less fortunate had to appear before the Means Test Panel in an office on Radford Road at its junction with Silverdale Road.

Council Housing (11)

At the end of the war the government had been concerned that 41% of men called up for military service had medical problems attributed to poor housing. They declared a policy of 'Homes fit for heroes'. Nottingham's Housing Department under its Surveyor, Cecil Howitt, immediately set about utilising the subsidies becoming available. Wide acres of farm-land remained in Basford for his purpose. Earlier housing had relied upon private investors filling small plots. This had led to low standards and poor planning. Scullery, coalhouse and outside lavatory reaching out into a common back yard had left many a living room deprived of sunlight for most of the day. Moreover a density of fifty or even a hundred houses to the acre was no longer acceptable

New housing was to be at twenty per acre or as low as twelve on new estates. Each house was to have a minimum of 70' between its front and the front of the house opposite and as the carriageways were only 14' to 16' wide - car-ownership was not foreseen - the result tended at first to bring long front gardens with smaller back ones. Roads were to follow contours, mature trees be preserved and there were to be allotments and grassed open spaces for children to play on.

Inside the houses, living rooms were planned for maximum daylight and an open fire heating water for the sink and bathroom was coupled with a modern cooking range. Thoughtfully, there was to be room either side of the fireplace for an arm-chair. One could see the ideal of father smoking his pipe and reading the newspaper with mother opposite knitting.

The scullery was kept deliberately small to stop it being used as a living room. It was equipped with a gas copper, gas cooker and deep sink with draining boards. Room was left for mangle and wash tub so that they weren't left outside.

Houses of the 'parlour' type had the bathroom upstairs, but in the smaller ones, usually called a 'single' it was on the ground floor. Each house had to have a linen store over the hot-water cylinder, a lavatory near the back door, and a larder with a stone slab and zink screen over its window. There was to be an entrance hall at the front and a coal house at the back to hold one ton of coal.

As a rough guide, rents were set at one third of an unskilled labourer's wage, but later this was reduced to one quarter. Applicants had to be Nottingham residents with wages below a certain level, married and able to produce satisfactory character references. Despite the cost and many restrictions, there were immediately 2027 families on the waiting list.

The first Council houses were built at Sherwood. Four on Woodville Drive were completed in June, 1920 at a cost of £844 each. Fourteen more were built on Sunrise Avenue in February 1922, followed by another group on Dornoch Avenue.

Stockhill Estate

Larger developments were already planned. The first true estate, was planned in November, 1919 for 31 acres at Stockhill. 225 houses there were occupied by May, 1922. A road planned from Broad Walk across to Bar Lane was abandoned to leave room for the Ellis and Guilford Schools opened in 1929.

Sherwood Estate

The City's housing triumph of the period, though, was the Sherwood Estate designed on 'garden city' lines, a name adopted by a public house nearby. Valley Road was extended from Hucknall Road to reach Mansfield Road in 1926 and 127 acres south of it were bought. To speed the building, several contractors were used and by June, 1923 665 houses were occupied between Edwards Lane and Mansfield Road. West of Edwards Lane 70 private houses and 422 council houses filled the rest of the site by June 1924 with space left for a school. Housing representatives from other councils and from Europe came to see the project.

Several families with salaries above the limit were found to be living on the estate. They were instructed to move elsewhere.

Liddington Street

Two terraces of fourteen houses were built and occupied on Liddington Street, New Basford about the same time, but they were unpopular and the experiment was not repeated.

Highbury Estate

After the embankment and viaducts of the Great Northern Line were built from Daybrook to Cinderhill it was commonly thought that the area beyond was in Bulwell. In fact, part of Highbury Hospital and Bagnall at Cinderhill were in

45

Basford as those wishing to marry at a church were to discover.

Much of the new Highbury Estate, 376 houses built on 30 acres between 1922 and 1937, was in Basford. The houses cost £300 each, were rented at 7/3d (about 36p)per week plus rates. They were specifically intended for poorly-paid ex-servicemen.

Aspley Estate

To the west, the parish boundary followed Bells Lane, to Broxtowe Hall, thence across Aspley to the top of the present Melbourne Road, then along a stream across the Bluecoat school grounds down to the Leen near Bobbers Mill. By 1930 1200 houses of the Aspley Estate were there, followed by the Crane School. 'Parlour houses' cost £308 to build with £295 for 'singles'. Like Sherwood it was a source of civic pride with visitors from home and abroad to see it. By August, 1930 the City had secured a compulsory purchase order against the Edge Estate for land up to Aspley Lane and a further 1680 dwellings were ready by March, 1932 to complete the project.

Heathfield Estate

The two former bleach-yard reservoirs on Valley Road, above and below the railway embankment, were filled in mainly with ashes from the Basford incinerator, and the Day Brook was piped, Beyond the embankment, 564 houses became the Heathfield Estate by July, 1932, and Barlock Road area was privately developed soon afterwards.

Whitemoor Estate

About the same time, the Duke of Newcastle gave land for Western Boulevard across the White Moor. The Leen and railway beside the church were again bridged, Fairfax Street was widened to become part of Valley Road and the city ringroad took shape. On farmland and allotments up to High street(Basford Road)the council built 576 houses by 1933. Barnes family's Churchfields farm house, behind Bailey Street medical centre was demolished. Whitemoor Road which had linked Nuthall Road and Mill-in-the Hole with Alpine Street was broken at the top of Bailey Street.

Other housing areas

Other areas in the parish were developed, such as Bells Lane between the Basford quarry and Broxtowe Hall. Here the land was built up with ashes from the Eastcroft incinerator. Small housing developments, some private, such as Perry Road and at Sherwood were built in the late twenties and early thirties. House-building was taking place elsewhere in Nottingham at this time but Basford led the way. In less than twenty years between the two World Wars every piece of farm land there had been developed and thousands of people housed to the highest standards of the time.

Only ten years before the Second World War flocks of sheep from either side of Valley Road were driven to market across the 1832 Leen bridge at Church Street for loading into railway trucks. Cattle were taken along Vernon Road and Church Street to slaughter houses behind the Cinderhill Co-operative shop and at Mellor's butchers at the bottom of Cowley Street. Traffic volumes now make this seem incredible.

Between the wars few people were able to buy their own houses, most lived in rented terraces and dreamt of rising to the top of the housing list. In Nottingham the ring road, Council House and the new estates, though valuable assets in themselves were also introduced to make work at a time of depression.

Schools

In 1870 School Boards had, at last, brought compulsory education for those outside church schools. Seven years later schools were built on Haydn Road and Radford Road. The following year Percy Street school was built at a cost of £10,000. Into the new century schools looking remarkably like factories were established at Southwark Street and Hucknall Road to be followed in 1911 and 1912 by smaller ones at Scotland Place, now Heathfield, Haydn Road and Scotholm. These last were in time to become emergency hospitals for war wounded.

The Ellis School, built 1928

In 1928, at the instigation of Henry Whipple, Director of Education, a new style of elementary school was built on   Bar Lane, the Ellis block for boys and the Guilford for girls. Each school was in the style of a Roman villa with central lawns surrounded by classrooms, each catering for 400 pupils aged 10 to 14 years.

Others on similar lines were built in the next few years, Haywood on Perry Road, at Aspley the Crane in 1933 and shortly before the Second World War, the Whitemoor School.

Chapter Seven

The Second World War - 1939 to 1945 - and afterwards

The Second World War and the years immediately following brought national problems of survival but with no real change in the face of Basford. Fortunately, the parish had suffered little from enemy bombing: war casualties at home and in the forces had been much lower than in the Great War. But as post- war shortages disappeared and returning servicemen settled to civilian life some changes did take place.

Public Transport Post War

The trams on the Mansfield Road, Nottingham Road and Radford Road routes had been superceded by trolley buses by 1936. The first were known as 'trackless' with solid tyres and an open staircase at the rear. During the sixties these were replaced by diesel buses leading to the decline of the railways. The Suburban Line had closed between the wars, and in the sixties the Great Northern and Great Central lines through the parish followed. The line to Mansfield, by the church, remained mainly for moving coal and the busy goods yard was gradually taken over by other businesses. The stations in the parish closed, except for Vernon Road which lasted but a little longer. Cast-iron slot machines for chocolate bars and a device for stamping letters onto aluminium strips were to be sadly missed.

More Houses

Houses, some council, some privately built, soon filled pockets of land which remained unused in Sherwood, on Arnold Road and on the steep hillside off Valley Road opposite the Heathfield Estate. Into the sixties, seventies and eighties Victorian dwellings and factories above North Gate were demolished, with new houses and business parks taking their place. The departure of the railways with their stations, cuttings, viaducts and embankments opened up surprisingly large areas, again mostly taken for house-building. Saxby's works with twin chimneys on the sky-line at Bar Lane disappeared to give way for houses as did the bleachworks of Cox and Widdowson on Vernon Road. Carrington Market Place with its surrounding terraces was cleared to make room for a school. Ashwell's bleachyard remained but to house a timber merchant, making the Vernon Road Bleaching Company the last of its type in the parish. Shipstone's extensive premises awaited development but the gasworks site could find no buyer until the chemicals poisoning its soil had been neutralised.

Basford Town

Landmarks such as bridges over Valley Road and Vernon Road disappeared but without doubt the major change was the demolition of Basford Town with its bustling shops and services centred on Lincoln Street. Some 18.9 acres of Victorian housing on the hillside between Percy Street and Lincoln Street were cleared and Queen Street, West Gate, Wicklow Street, and Brown's Croft, together with a number of terraces were wiped from the map. With the shops went banks, public houses, offices and the works of Noah Hopewell, builder and maker of hosiery machinery. The houses had been unfit by present day standards, but breaking-up and moving long- established communities brought social problems.

Apart from a few small shops backing onto the Leen on Lincoln Street, the area was cleared by 1962 and by 1971 822 Bison wall-framed homes filled the site. They took the shape of 17 residential blocks rising to five or eight floors, with four tower blocks of 18 or 19 storeys. Walk-ways linked the structures and ample car parking space was provided. But there were no new shops.

The basic design of the flats was good but the workmanship was poor in some cases leading to dampness, leaking roofs and condensation. In addition, a major danger was exposed at Ronan Point flats in London. An explosion had been caused by improperly connecting a gas cooker to the mains showing structures could collapse if one panel should fail. The blocks had to be reinforced causing inconvenience to the residents many of whom had been rehoused from elsewhere. The flats were unpopular, they had no future, and by 1985 the hillside was again covered with rubble.

Eddie Mellors, a retired butcher and member of a long- established Basford family, lived nearby. He watched the demolition of the old houses, the flats going up, their coming down and preparations being made for traditional housing all within fourteen years. The towers which had dominated the valley had been an unwelcome and costly exercise. Their removal was a relief but Lincoln Street shopping centre was not replaced and the line of small business units on the old part of Nottingham Road leading to it did not enhance the scene.

Clover Green

From 1986 onwards, in place of the flats, 301 dwellings, bungalows, houses, and warden-aided apartments were built to a good traditional design. There was a mix of public and private funding, with some for rent and others for sale. The community centre from the days of the flats was retained and another built for the residents of a warden-aided complex, Clover Green. Bacon's Field, 3.2 acres beside the Leen was kept for recreation.

The Leen Improvement Scheme

For centuries the winding nature of the Leen within the parish had caused floods.

In 1962 a solution was found. A new channel with bends only at Vernon Park was dug beside the railway from Bulwell to Mill-in-the- Hole and beyond. Mill races at Mill Street and Lincoln Street were by-passed and the junction of the Daybrook and Leen moved to conform. It has probably solved the problem of flooding, but the scene is stark.

1960s - Junction of Leen and Daybrook,

Willow Holt and Sycamore Grange

The former playing field of Basford United beside the Leen at Mill Street has now been raised by several feet, and dwellings on piles are being built. This estate, behind the ruins of the mill is to be known as Willow Holt, no doubt recalling Scaling's plantation.

By 1997 the park-land of Basford Hall has become a housing estate called Sycamore Grange. Two hundred years ago Robert Hall (Junior) bought the field, then called Raw Wong, for his house.

Nature Reserve

One large open space now remains. It lies between Western Boulevard and Radford Road. There is a nature reserve between the allotment gardens and the church. The future of the rest, formerly the gasworks railway sidings, has not been decided. Beneath its weeds and brambles lies Thomas Hawksley's Scotholme Reservoir of 1827.

Basford People, Businesses and Buildings

Buildings such as Basford House, Basford Hall, Churchfields, Sycamore Hall, and Algarthorpe deserve researching as do businesses such as the Vernon Road Bleaching Company, Shipstones, Meridian and Jardines

In his 1914 book, *"Old and New Basford - Then and Now "* Robert Mellors gives thumb-nail biographies of the worthies of his day. Since then there has been no shortage of people or families with local connections who have made their mark in the locality or in the city. Indeed, George Brough with his Brough Superior motor cycles in the 1920s and 1930s was a national figure in the eyes of those who admired his most powerful of machines. Lawrence of Arabia was a frequent visitor to his workshop on Haydn Road and bought several. He was riding one at the time of his death. Brough's works moved to Vernon Road where they remained until the Second World War diverted them to war work. He lived at the top of Llanberis Grove; the house has gone but the lodge, a bungalow, remains at the bottom of the Grove.

In service to the people of the parish, mention has to be made of Doctor Charles Hill of Churchfields, Bailey Street, a general practitioner married to a daughter of Charles Cox, bleacher of Rock House. His commitment to his patients was widely acknowledged. He died whilst attending one and was greatly missed. His dispenser, Lawrence Lunn, a member of a local family, was equally well-known and is happily still living in the parish.

John Lowndes, MA, a Cambridge Rowing Blue, a man of outstanding size and personality was Vicar of Basford from 1930 for more than thirty years whilst John Marlow, herbalist with his shop on Lincoln Street is remembered for his support of the Queensbury Baptist Church. Another Lincoln Street shopkeeper was George Frederick Godson, chemist and churchwarden: a man of great dignity and presence. In a room behind his shop hung a certificate that he had attended a course on dentistry and many had cause to recall their experiences in his chair.

George Spencer, who lived in Basford Town as a boy, opened a factory in the 1920s on Bar Lane making hosiery under the name 'Vedonis', an apt contraction of the names of Venus and Adonis.

Joseph Bates, manager of the New Basford firm of machine builders, Swift and Wass, was an amateur player for the Forest Football Club when he moved to Dagenham in the 1880s. There he worked for the Woolwich Arsenal gun factory, joining a factory team. He secured a gift of shirts from his old team thereby making red the colour of both professional clubs.

Noah Hopewell lived on Lincoln Street in a house adjoining his works. His firm was well established as builders, makers of hosiery finishing machinery and carts.

He was well-known for his support of youth groups, especially the 44th Nottingham Scouts.

The teaching profession with its vital contribution to the country's future deserves a mention. There are, no doubt, many outstanding characters to be recalled such as the dynamic William Arthur Grainger, first headmaster of the Ellis.

Giving a few names invites criticism on behalf of those omitted but no-one will challenge a mention of two who lived here, Jane Torvill and Christopher Dean.

SOURCES

HM Prison,Nottingham, 1891-1991, a short history. (Prison Service Publication)

T. Bailey. Annals of Nottinghamshire. History of the County of Nottingham,including the Borough. (Nottingham, 1853)

C. Bartholomew. The Leen Valley.(W.J.Butler and Co. Nottingham, 1983)

J. Beckett. The Book of Nottingham. (Barracuda Books, Buckingham, 1990) (Ed,) DEA Centenary History of Nottingham (Manchester University Press, 1997)

E. Bryson, Portrait of Nottingham, (Nottingham, 1974)

M. Caplan, Poor Law in Nottinghamshire, (Transactions of the Thoroton Society, Vol.LXX1V, 1970)

J.D.Chambers, Nottinghamshire in the 18th Century, (P.S.King and Sons, London, 1932)

R.A.Church, Economic and Social Change in a Midland Town: Victorian Nottingham, 1815-1900, (Cass and Co., London, 1966)

A. Cossons,The Turnpike Roads of Nottinghamshire. (Historical Association Leaflet No. 97, 1934)

T. Felkin, History of the Machine Wrought Hosiery and Lace Manufacturers. (Nottingham, 1867)

T. Fry. The History of Sherwood, a Nottingham Suburb. (Nottingham, 1989)

D. Gray. Nottingham - Settlement to City.(Nottingham Co- operative Society, 1953)

D. Lowe and J. Richards, The City of Lace, (Nottingham Lace Centre. 1982); William Lee and Lace, (Nottingham Lace Centre, 1989)

S.N.Mastoris and S.M.Groves, (Eds,) Sherwood Forest in 1609. A Crown Survey by Richard Bankes.(Thoroton Society Record Series VolXL1992/3)

R. Mellors, Old and New Basford, Then and Now (J. and H. Bell, Nottingham, 1913)

J. Morris, (Ed.) Domesday Book, -28- Nottinghamshire, (Phillimore, Chichester, 1977)

G. Oldfield, A History of Basford Rural District Council,1894-1974,(Knapp,Nottingham, 1974)

J.F. Phillips, Town and Village in the 19th Century, Nottingham and Nottinghamshire Villages, (University of Nottingham, 1973)

D.E.Roberts,DEThe Nottingham Gas Undertaking, 1818- 1949. (East Midlands Gas, 1980)

K.S.S.Train, St. Leodegarius Church, Basford, Nottingham.(Service Publications, Ltd, Shoreham by Sea, 1976)

G. Trease, Nottingham, A Biography.(The Amethyst Press, Otley, 1984)

R.E.A.Wells, Riot and Political Disaffection in Nottinghamshire in the Age of Revolutions, 1776-1803. (University of Nottingham, 1983)

Other sources; newspapers, directories, manuscripts.

Maps and Illustrations

Kind permission to reproduce those maps and illustrations marked (NCCLS) has been given by the Nottinghamshire County Council Leisure Services and those marked (BLHS) has been given by the Basford and District Local History Society.

Erratum
p.41. The photograph of Valley Road
bridge was taken by Henry E. Crooks
in 1937

Nottinghamshire
Heritage Series -

BELL TALES *by Stan Smith*

FOR CONSPICUOUS GALLANTRY - Local V.C. Holders - *by N. McCrery*

HISTORY OF SUTTON IN ASHFIELD - *facsimile of 1907 edition*

LORD BYRON *" Mad, bad and dangerous to know."*- *by E. Eisenberg*

NOTTINGHAMSHIRE STRET TO STREET GUIDE .

THE OLD NORTH ROAD *by Joan Board*
A TO Z OF PILGRIM COUNTRY *by Joan Board*

WOLLATON HALL *by Elizabeth May*
Wollaton as a family home and Natural History Museum

SOME NOTTINGHAMSHIRE PUB STORIES *by Stan Smith*

COUNTRY POETRY *by Leslie Williamson*

MARY & WILLIAM - a north Midland couple *by Joy Dunicliff*

BASFORD - Village to Suburb *by A.S.Bowley*